Past Life Press

# Observations of a Dead Man ...

Steffan Piper

"I might have to bite the bullet ... but that doesn't mean I want to eat the rifle."
- Keanu Reeves

Other works by the Author:

*Novels:*

    Yellow Fever
    Waiting for Andre
    Greyhound
    Exit

*Poetry Compilations:*

    Electronic Butterflies
    Observations of a Dead Man
    During the Apocalypse ...

ISBN: **9780615142708**

Copyright © 2007 by Past Life Press.

All rights reserved. Printed in the United States of America.

No part of this book may be used or reproduced in any manner Whatsoever without written permission except in the case of brief quotations embodied in critical articles and reviews.

9 8 7 6 5 4 3 2 1

Observations of a Dead Man ...

Consciously Becoming
The Fabled Hero
Of the New World

Taking us all
Carefully there
In reverse …

Observations of a dead man
From a world in which all is lost
Watching all this unfold daily
From across an expanding ocean
As vast as a plate of glass

I'm unable to touch you
I'm unable to reach out to you
I'm separated from this world
That has become only a shadow
Now only a figment

I can see my reflection in the glass
And it's as close to me as a shop window
I can see the darkness reflected from my eye
Trying to find its way home
Watching the white glint of my teeth, I'm smiling
    Knowing that it'll soon be over
        Knowing that when I fall back into sleep …
    you'll be waking

Mine is to wait until you dream

So here I lay
Dormant
Breathing
Isolated
Somehow
Alive

You can feel the transfer
Within a handshake
All that bad intent

Stuck in a n elevator with you
You were fantasizing about
Having bawdy sex with your
Japanese neighbor's wife

During that conversation over the phone you thought
To yourself
That I was a prick and that
You wished I would die
And leave you your inheritance

Sometimes ...

I really wish I was the devil incarnate.
Listening to people's evil thoughts would bring me joy.
But I'm not
And you can almost see their words stream across their dull
Grey faces as they pass you in droves
Out in the streets.

I can hear you when you open your mouth
And I can hear you even when you don't
Some people might say it's a gift or power
But it's not
It's hell.
All I can do is hear you and not respond.
All the things I would want to tell you but cannot.

If I could just tell you that everything wasn't as bad as you're telling yourself
If I could just tell you that soon - it will pass
If I could tell you to look me in the eye and understand you'd see
But I can't.

At least, if I lived in a world that understood, I wouldn't feel so alone.

Every time I look in the mirror
There are several things
I'd rather not see
Myself for one
The world around me
Another
And the absolute lack of you
The last

This is not the world
In which I find
Much solace
No friend
No comfort nor vice
And nowhere to turn

This is not the world into
Which I was born

This is me ... is that you?


John Wayne –

This is me. Is that you?
I heard you're in hell now
How's the food?
Did they set you up with a ranch and a hay barn?
Do you spend time riding charred souls
    into the lake of fire?


I saw your reflection in plate glass
    While walking the strip in downtown Palm Springs
It was 120 degrees out
But you were shivering and looking for an open flame
Hoping to keep warm

I was told:
    They didn't care too much for Hondo down there either ...
    That they no longer call you 'The Duke' ...
    That you've shacked up with obese Englishman ...
    That you love to watch porno in the afternoons ...
    And that on Sundays you go to church
    And play horseshoes with Heinrich Himmler


I was told all the flesh on your corpulent frame melted
And you now appear
As black
As a burnt marshmallow
Imagine the irony
Imagine your friends


Palm Springs is the only place on Earth
That's close enough to Hell where
Sometimes you cross over
You looked fine to me
But maybe it was just a disguise
Maybe it was my mind

You were trying to tell me that
Someone I knew was sorry
That they wanted to apologize
You were mumbling and coughing over my shoulder
Like you had pneumonia and it was winter


I stopped and watched you in the reflection
Of the Starbucks window-glass


People inside thought I'd lost my mind
They thought I was talking to myself
They couldn't see you, or probably didn't want to
That's okay, I don't blame them


Tell the son of a bitch I don't want an apology
Lottery numbers are better proof that he feels my pain
I doubt he'd comply
He wouldn't do anything that would make his soul burn hotter
Especially not for me


I'm getting awful tired of running into you like this …
Out on the street, and on my way to dinner
I can only speak in code so much before I'm completely bored
People might begin to talk
I was never a fan, nor did I enjoy your filmic detritus
You probably would've blacklisted me as well
    Had I known you then


I read a book about you in High School
It said you were a jackass to a lot of people
Including your family
I guess you got what you deserved
You were made moot from unseen fall-out
It completed you
It absorbed you
The nuclear winter of your own private Utah


They ripped your chest in half

When they harvested your soul

Your limbs dangled from the side board
And your expression wilted
Did you taste the juice …
    When they embalmed you?
Did you feel the floor drop out …
    When they convicted you?

Tell me …
John Wayne
This is me
Is that you?

Sometimes I'd rather drink Mezcal ...


The night started off badly
I broke a disc into a million tiny pieces
I chased the end of a Mexican nightmare
Everything went from bad to absolutely shitty
In seconds ... and it wasn't even seven-thirty

One thing that I can say for sure
Is that
Quite simply
I haven't been the same since
The veil of the world has thinned around me
And opened
A reality that was once just a dim path
Is now a hand with claws.
A bear-trap around my fucking ankle.

Perhaps it was only my soul coming home from vacation
I awoke on the floor
Clutching the vast expanse of the porcelain bowl
Covered in blood, puke and the smell of gasoline.

The scenes lasted only moments and then vanished like a wave
Receding back into the tide ... then gone.
A black asphalt bruise traversed the edge of my chest looking strangely like
The edge of my household toilet
I carried that war-wound for over a week.
Unsure of every story and phone call that assaulted me days after.

The appliance grip of
   dear life that keeps us
   between a vision
Of what we've always had
And what we're about to lose.

The temptation to push down on the silver handle just beyond my periphery
and clear the stomach filled air around me is more than tempting.
To live in this continuous squalor seems to be what I've decided.
But sometimes, sometimes, I'd rather die. Damn it.

Why do I believe in brotherhood
    When I am surrounded by adversaries?

Why do I believe in brotherhood
    When I'm taking the sniper's blast
        In the face – through the chest – and in the back
        From across the cesspool of my fetid friends?

Why do I believe in brotherhood
    In a city like Los Angeles
        That sells souls as if they were
        Cheap plastic bags that you might put your bullshit in?

Why do I believe in brotherhood
    In a country like the United States
        When gang-bangers are taking money bets
        to see who'll gut me first?

Why do I believe in brotherhood
    In a world such as this
        That sees only my credit report
        My social security number
        My wallet
        But not my face?

In this life
    As it sours in front of me
    And I age and become obsolete ...

Why do I believe in brotherhood?

Poetry is a code
That's moving through you
just below the surface

Poetry is not a sedative
For your next five minutes
It's not an opiate
In which our survival collides
These words are not meant for now –but later
Much later
When the push of your life, my life, this life
Becomes unbearable.
When all the politicians become unbearable
When everyone you've ever loved hates you
When every member of your family has left you,
Died on you in the night
Put you in a nursing home
Left you to rot in prison, jail or a hospital
Decided to ignore you because you work in a cubicle
Or despise you because you told them you were gay,
Madly in love with a Jewish American Princess or a
Young Republican

I've been hated my whole life
For one reason or another
They've always had their reasons
But here I am
Spending time with you
Sitting at the foot of my poetry in silence
Going over the code

Dead Mexican Artist ...

Ola chica,
    I see you ...

The reincarnation of a dead Mexican artist
The embodiment of another man's woman
The voice of a girl
who's trying hard to tell you something important
but stays silent
A whisper

The soft touch of a catholic icon in candle light
After a few drinks but no communion

The laugh of an alarm to remind me that the world's on fire
That I should evacuate the building
And that people still fall in love

You speak to me in a language that I can barely understand
And slowly, somehow, resurrect a part of my past
That is yet unlived and was never meant to rise

When you're near me, you're a sucker to hold my hand
And a sadist to hear me out
Excavating my refrigerator, you're beautiful in the morning
So patient in the afternoon and warm to touch at night
Alive, connected, and close by

I'm going to blow my brains out
at some disputed barricade
Self-loathing is not a strange bed-fellow
Having tea with my state-sponsored neighbor
I'm going to blow my brains out

I need to tell you
That this life
Isn't what you think
It's not what you've been told

This body is no more than a complex
Jail cell and my mind is nothing
More than a labyrinth made to
Distract me and burn time like
Blood spilling from my wrists
Drying in the sun like dust
Beneath me

I need to tell you
That this life
Isn't what you think
It's not what you've been told

These hands are practiced tools
Weapons that have been trained
To quickly choke the life from you
Slap you hard, awaken you
And send you reeling

This heart has been tempered
by the sharp point of many blades
That have pierced it and
Run it through
This heart has been set ablaze
In a single moment and then
Extinguished completely in the next
Disposed of *unshamed facedly*
and forgotten
Like packaging around some product
That you had wished
Wholeheartedly
That you hadn't spent money on.

My life equates to a refund
A merchandise return
A scratched off to-do list upon buck slip
Careless and forgotten

Klieg Light …

I saw my body
Burning in the Klieg light

Naked and pale blue
Stretched thin upon the table

Toe-tagged and ready to go
Awaiting new destinations

I saw my body burning
White flames of the Klieg light
Licking me, slowly, all over

A final kiss from this life
Before departing

Martha, My Dear …


Martha Stewart saved me
  from an almost inevitable suicide today.

I was sinking fast with my ice-cream scooper,
  a handful of very dark Dandelion greens,
    and a decorative jar of Persian Pearl tulips.

I didn't know if I could survive another day
  without guidance from the only living-god.

I didn't know if I would remember how to breathe
  and maintain that icy-cool that I've been trying so hard to emulate

I'll lose myself later once I get to the
  photos by Jose Manuel Picayo Rivera
    commands from her holiest of holies and that
      the sure-glazed thousand-yard stare of my daytime queen

What was I before her, how did I survive in this mess?
  What the hell was my purpose and what exactly was I doing with all those years following that idiot Maury Povich.

Everything was freeze-dried, drive-thru, black plastic
  Before I wised up and became a subscriber
    A follower, a K-mart debutante.

When they took you away, darling
    Did they force you to eat food from the microwave
      Wash with unfiltered water and store-bought bar-soap
        Did you eat scrambled eggs cooked on cheap Teflon with no olive oil?
Don't worry they'll pay for that
      They'll pay for what they did to you.

Allow me to make a supplication …
  For 15 minutes at four-fifty
    As I slowly drizzle one tablespoon
        of 'best-quality' tequila over the good-times,
          sprinkle with lime zest, and pass-out immediately;
            poolside.

In my other life I was
Steve McQueen
Wearing that German Army Officer's Uniform
Roaring away
On that borrowed motorcycle
Fuck you

What nuts he had
Ever seen 'em so big?

Blasting across the country side
In khaki's and a blue sweatshirt
My heart-raced
Without artificial stimulus
I thought my organ was going to explode

Just West of Unabomber ...


A Warning ... to all smug cunts, far and wide

Fuck off and die.
I've got enough rejection letters now
To qualify myself for an unabated
Tirade of cold, hard reality ...

First ... I would really like to wipe my ass with your Pulitzer Prize
I read your shit, last night while drunk, on the crapper
It stunk of fish head soup, burning tires in a war zone,
And a used condom in the steaming tropics
I'm speaking of your poetry – not my toilet.

But which would you rather prefer?
The corn that exploded into the porcelain void
From between my butt-cheeks?
Or another published critique
   on your "heartfelt" trite piece of "humanity"
   that made the rounds last year through the Nationals,
The Kenyon Review, The Missouri Press
And the all-absurds-paid-for Edward Albee Lecture Circuit?

Second ... If I hear your gushings, one more time
About "feeling so sparse", the "Uncanny Valley",
"Cartesian Scarecrows", "April morn" or
"My Beckettian Masturbation Tragedy"
I'll search far and wide for the Mossberg.
I'll polish the shells to a high shine
So they slide home with a whistle, chamber and click
Just so you know that I'm getting ready to unplug you
From your Poetic matrix, your Bethlehem Grid System,
And your tight, groupie, eighteen year old vagina and
Scatter your press-ready, fellowshipped, work-shopped brains
All over your fresh-smelling dry-cleaning

Go to hell you boring son-of-a-bitch,
You sick bastard

Take the next train to the edge of Lemming Field
Do us all a favor – And drop!

Anjelica Huston …

I was reading from an old journal
I found an entry I'd made and forgotten
Two pages – taped together with purpose

Surprised, I discovered that
Somewhere
I had lived a secret life
I was a boy and folded tightly into the arms
Of Anjelica Huston

She was the mother I never had
Her long inky hair brushing across my face
Turquoise jewelry against my neck and chest
She toweled me dry after swimming
I could see how much she loved me

David Bowie was playing upon loudspeakers
Palm trees swayed above us
trying to pull my attention away and distract me
I felt your smile beaming at me
From the distance of a mere foot

I must've been five
Standing transfixed in my dark-blue swim trunks
Cooling on drip-dry
You told me that I had to hurry
But I didn't want to leave
You'd be gone again and I'd be alone once more

When I awake from this I wonder how many more times it'll come
I wonder what I'm being told.
What I'm being shown and why.
Because of this, for years, I've loved you.
I guess you're the mother I've never known.

I think of you every time I hear 'life on mars'.

I want to time travel back to 1951
  and stab Harley Earl in the chest
    with the front bumper
      from a pearlescent silver
        convertible Nash-Healey.

I just cannot take another day
  or share another inch of
    this god forsaken earth
      with middle-aged men
        who feel it their duty
          to sport
            The Chevrolet Corvette

I hate Corvettes
I hate everything about them
I hate the stupid dull colors they paint them
I hate the stupid dull people that buy them,
I hate the cloned grey slaves that drive them
I hate middle-aged men with back hair in yellow polo neck's and
Steve McQueen turn-up's the drive by smiling.
That drive by douching.

I hate bald septuagenarians in shell suits and cheap gold clink
Trying to lure every slippery bimbo into his two door flaccid fantasy
Hoping to make young men squirm, old hags bark and bank-men proud

I hate Mexican auto-mechanics out for a lunch-time drive
Wasting tread
In another man's wet-dream
trying to beat a light, gun the pedal
or die trying.

Jesus, please fucking *save us*
    from this Corvette hell.

I want to travel forward in time
    and make damn sure
      that I'm never caught driving
        a Chevrolet Corvette.

## The Pitch Black Lifetime
*Supertramp series #01*

Stuck in the Laundromat at five am
I was lost in a world unknown
From the speaker above
Came the song – like a code
An activation of a moth-balled killer
The keywords tripped in combo

> *Goodbye stranger,*
> *It's been nice.*
> *Hope you'll find your*
> *Paradise.*

In a sweeping flush
My past rushed at me
From all sides, surrounding
In hibernation – I killed a man
A Glock 10mm – steady in hand
Porcelain innards
Teflon rounds
At a Starbucks in Prague
I gunned a man down

I felt betrayed folding socks
And dropping quarters into
The old metal abyss of my forgotten soul

> *Goodbye Mary,*
> *Goodbye Jane.*
> *Will we ever*
> *Meet again?*

I felt no sorrow, and felt no shame
About all the men I'd planted
That I'd never see again
I had no regrets about the political targets erased
The unknown little girl's mommies and daddies
I poisoned in foreign plazas over green tea and sushi

I'm a machine
Logical – digital – dependable
A man with a weapon
A nightmare in a pin-striped black suit
That I'll forget about in moments forward

I'm trying to tell you
What I've learned
I know how it sounds
It sounds absurd

Please tell me

I just don't know
Who I am

My memories have been removed
to protect the information
My life has been dissected and served back
After much careful consideration

> *Feel no sorrow,*
> *Feel no shame.*
> *Come tomorrow,*
> *Feel no pain.*

But when the words come down
From the command line interrupt
A DOS prompt in the back-brain
Network Addressing at its finest
A Carriage Return Execution
Sleeper cell caressing
The code awakes me, sends me
The church mouse husband
Camouflaged in my front room
Evolves into the *Treadstone* killer
In the full moon.

> *Tried to see your*
> *Point of view*
> *Hope your dreams*
> *Will all come true*

We don't always lose …


Brynner and McQueen
   How 'bout that?
      'Gently, boys, gently'

Into your long forgotten nights
   Huffing liquid asbestos
      And smoking cigarettes

Trading the moments of your fragile lives
   For the silent relief from that moment in front
      Building momentum and building speed
         It didn't matter that you built men for years to come
         And you gave your soul like others give ashes
            Blowing over the land
            Then gone

Were you ever really here at all?
   Or were you really just the biggest work of fiction I've known?
      Can't be.

Vios con dios, Amigos

   We don't always lose …

Out on the fray …

My life is more than just a redundant collection
    of moves witnessed and forgotten.
My life is not just another version
    of Dr. Zhivago on a widescreen, muted.
My life is not just a poorly executed chess game
    where all the pawns have been sacrificed
    all the rooks smoke crack on the corner
    all the knights are jockeying oblique positions
    Just to get next to some ethnic queen

And I'm stuck moving in slow motion,
Out on the fray
In enemy territory
Moving Slowly
One thought at a time

They say that
Every game of chess
    is often ruled by its opening
Every move has a consequence
Every advance forces a fallback
Every mistake costs life

And every prize takes sacrifice
That's the nature of it

Desperate
   And on the run
Hot on my heels
   I feel like Al Cowlings
      Running head-long into the afterlife

The hiss of demons on my tail
   is deafening
     I've got my foot

      Buried
    Straining for dear-life

      Pushing like a bitch
     On the pedal

That sonofabitch Simpson is laughing
   Gaining on me
     Dragging the knife blade
     Behind him
       Across concrete

Someone thought they heard something
A knock on the AC unit out back

I'm losing in the battle for
   A clean getaway

I'm lost in the battle
   For a clean yesterday

I'm waiting for my heart to give out
Even though it probably already has
I'm waiting for it to fail
Under pressure from the weight of
The world resting upon it
It feels like a stone inside my chest
Ready to drop
It feels heavy and cold
And almost as if someone is holding it
In their hands, crushing it

My wife Mini
Has the heart of an accountant
And the soul of a clerk-typist

Her fist balls up and shakes
Like a stone in a tin can
Like a boulder falling from a cliff
Through the air unimpeded

Staring you down
Is a full-time job

So, Keith Merritt wrote that poem
   I was astounded at what he said
      Just the idea, alone …
    Steve McQueen making it
    Clearing the barb
In an alternate reality
  It happened
He wasn't high, and so he ascended
   Lifting up over the fence
   then landing on the other side
     When Keith said:
       "Steve stopped –
       Turned around
       Lit a smoke
       Kick started it in the ass
       and rode off"

Goddamn what a scene
      That would've been

           Quite a sight

My Wiener Dog ...

Blistering hot
The Burbank sun is baking the slaves
   out for their sick gravy lunches
Studio executives who dress
    like all their clothes came from
    Wal-Mart or their filthy old uncle
    who smelled of sour milk and
    never washed his clothes

My Wiener Dog wants to kill these people
Almost as badly as I do
She stares ... fixated and intense
Watching the day-time soap trolls passing on the sidewalk
If she could rip their face off
   and bury them in a shallow grave
She'd feel actualized
She'd smile, bark and patrol the windows

I watch the madness unfold everyday
    from the comfort and breadth of my large white sofa
    In my Californian two-bedroom
    plastic and plaster labyrinth
      My wooden wind chime
        Dangling
          Like a dried corpse
            Drying in the sun
              Blowing in the crisp, hot winter wind
              Of this eighty degree world
              With clear skies

Screaming Police sirens
  In the distance
    looking long and wide
      for an old girlfriend

My Wiener Dog would chew on strychnine and slurp whiskey
  If I asked her to

We find strange ways to cope
  We find strange ways to live

We find strange ways to breed
    In this nightmarish and dark landscape of a city

We find different ways of getting through
  This bone-bleached world of
    hustlers, travelers and salesmen
      selling the world, pimping radiation, hustling a bone bleach

All of you whores
  reading this now
    consuming the planet
      like there's a fucking back-up

My Wiener Dog
  Will end all of you

A prelude to a world gone mad
Another reason to shoot myself
While using a silencer

Enough already

J.S. Bach is rolling in his grave
Turning like a rotisserie chicken
The sound of the burning spit is killing
Everything now falling on deaf ears and hot coals

He's made a list of transgressions
While partnered with Henry Miller
They're determined to see us in hell
Charbroiled and honey-glazed

Unfulfilled
They would be
As they feasted upon my loins

The sound of gunfire
The pitch of a diesel engine
The whine of a goddamn siren
The Moan of Englebert Humperdink
The reverberation of a top-forty station
Techno music from across the hall

No forgiveness tonight

The world is now abaft in the miasma
Of static and silence

I've always wanted to be a priest
Wear the collar
I'd thought about being a psychologist
Manning the chair – cross-legged
But the guilt was killing
The thought of
Rising
To unknown levels of hypocrisy
New heights

How could I give solace and pray?
How could I counsel and heal?

When every minute of the day
I'm cementing my own suicide
I would've slit my wrists
Swallowed pills ad infinitum

Confined to the sidelines
For just dreaming about it

A note to Frank Reardon ...

I went to Ferlinghetti's and ended up getting stuck upstairs, bro.
Just hoping to slip into the reverie of poetic history and days gone by.

I was caught in the midst of self-indulgent bullshit
Rehashed posturing of dressed-down salon queens
from New York City in the eighties
who were living within the socialite reality
of going balls deep into every random man
upon the coat-pile
    "until the plague started taking all our friends by the numbers."

I wanted to scream heresy, treason, theft, something ...
I wanted to set fire to the moderator ...
Not because you couldn't annunciate the poetry
you were garbling, reading, aping, coveting, publishing,
but because you were afraid to speak words like
Combivir, Acyclovir, miasma, chaos, baby grand or ripped condoms.

I was disgusted at the stink filling the small room with the windows closed.
The unwashed and unawakened masses that haven't found toothpaste or dial soap or the benefit of a fucking job.

The Goddamned burnouts clucking, clicking, nodding, laughing, spitting "oh yeah" and "oh yes" and "right, right" every time Algar name-dropped a cheap and over used pop-culture reference that was played out in 1987 like: *'Permanently confused like Jim from Taxi'.*

All I wanted was a copy of Neal Cassidy's stuff from the top shelf near the edge that wasn't anywhere on the net or in stores. I wanted to be a fucking cheap consumer not a pseudo-burnt-toast intellectual.

I made a weak attempt to rescue the print media ~ but couldn't get around the poetry Nazi's trying to spoon-feed me AIDS tales via a horde of fucking 'yes men' who were guffawing at the never ending ramble about Miguel dressing up in drag on ward G9 and humping the hole in his greasy hand at night with pictures of Ernast Fucking Borgnine.

*Jesus, I wanted to commit seppuku ...*

Maybe fag-hag queen hustlers slipping from the cold coil loudly makes me want to vomit in the face of the studio apartment man who publishes his own Amazon Reviews like a fucking narcissist. Maybe it's me.

Paul Weller & God in discussions to turn off the machine tonight ...


When the Style Council
   become the soundtrack
     for Starbucks consumers
       at six am
         I want out ...

When the only thing to watch
   On every goddamned channel
     Is Anna Nicole Smith
       Sean Hannity and MASH
   I want out ...

When all the overhead Muzak
   Is raping Stevie Winwood
     Aping The Police
       Van Morrison or
         Bruce Hornsby and the Range
     I want out ...

When the country is struggling
   To fit neatly and quietly
     Into the status quo
       For selfish reasons of their own
     I want out ...

When the only person I care about
   Is myself and yet I don't
     Have a clue as to
       Who I am
         I want out ...

When the snow caps are finished
   The polar bears are a myth and dusted
     When the Dolphins declare:
       *So long, and thanks for all the fish*
         I'll be out.

Fulang-Chang and I …


Café au lait
Valentine's day
Chinese New Year
San Francisco – somewhere in between

The burnt sky
The dry gutters
The world flashing starkly
Through the windows
Of Café De le Presse

My grey suit
My black tie
Your pink scarf
Your high heeled tennis-shoes that
Covered your bare feet
I heard prayers silently
From the people all around me

They didn't know how quickly
All their desires
Had been answered
When you came

Here I am watching 'Hannibal'
Supposedly the world's awake.
   Its daylight hours just inches away from me
       protected by concrete and plaster,
          a door, a dead-bolt and plenty of cash
The sound of the television is humming
Drowning the dull din of the slaves in the streets ,,,
Just inches away
Bach's Goldberg Aria is wafting above
   watching the patterns of the Persian rug below
       Tinkering away towards me
      Like small spiders across
      My downstairs apartment ceiling

What is it that we find so fascinating about an anti-hero,
   who dines on the free-range rude?
What is it that makes us elevate dullards
    and liars to positions above us?
       To control us?
What makes us dirty our hands
    and blacken our souls for
       those who would slovenly turn their backs
         and let us perish without pity?

Should I start peeling off my face and feed it to the dogs?
Well, damn it, if that aint entertainment.

What's the difference between good and evil
     when the world is working overtime
       to erase the definitions and make you live everyday
       like the ending of a movie
       where the bad guy saves the day,
       the seductress runs off with the money
       or everything you ever thought
       Was wrong?

Lawsuit …

All the Hollywood actors today
Are useless turds …

Spent pieces of jet trash
Blowing in the poetic vain

Brought to you in a neo-pseudo
Brylcreem and Lanolin state of perfection

All the starlets have pushed their way now
Through the myriad maze of
Casting-couch cock-sucking

Having found the 'Burgeoning Me'
At acting schools across the valley
Run by
Hacks
Charlatans
And profiteers

All seeking, arms extended the dripping
Wet booty of another naive bimbo
At places like
Gene Bua
Stella Adler
Steve Austin
The Actors Lab
The Actors Gym
The Actors Studio

And every other goddamned incarnation possible
Even the ugly ones are dressed down salon queens
Who could all easily have
An axe-handled pecker
Awaiting your tight-dime-anus
Hidden beneath the folds of her
Couture and high heeled attire

Again ...


Next time I get abducted
Please don't bring me back

Consider this notice official

Do with me what you will
As so many have already done
Probed and Questioned

Without permission

I could do without most
Of what this world has to offer
In all its scenic splendor

Don't save any piece of me, large or small
For Cesar to render

Jesus Christ, I haven't witnessed
Enough mutilations, cosmetic surgeries
Wife-swapping and genetic adaptations

Next time I get abducted
Please don't bring me back
Consider this a declarative salutation!

Everything is just beyond my reach
All things have now exceeded my grasp
And yet I'm asleep and empty-handed
What a fool I was to believe
I could survive this long without you

And how the world
just loves
a silly love song

Thank God for Bill Burroughs
Thank God, for old Bull Lee
   Hold onto that cane, Bill
   Hold onto that trust fund

Smile broadly and blaspheme
While I account for you
On this adding machine
And have a beer
And wipe the sweat from across my body

Thank God for the spirit
   In the corner of my eye
Thank God, for the spirit
   quietly explaining
   How to lie

The Pig-Bed ...

She went to Ikea
And bought herself a new bed
They call it a 'Hogbo'
What the hell are they thinking in Sweden?
New ways to laugh at fat Americans

Nice little Hogbo
Silent and sound
She's got her Famous potatoes
With some scrambled man eggs
And a side of guy gravy
Saved up in condoms beneath the bed

The turkey baster awaits
If you know what I mean

She's having herself a meal
A midnight snack
There she goes
The girl-interrupted
One more gorilla
Reports to the mist

Falling asleep in a food coma
Having herself one more sex-starved nightmare
Plaintively giving birth at dawn
To a much-beloved
Three-coil-steamer

Crispin Hellion Glover
   How else should this start?
I saw you today on the television
You were like Jesus on crack
Moses ... reclining in first class
With cool blonde broads
    And a martini

Holy Fuck
I couldn't believe my ears
Tesla was stirring curiously in his grave
From the deep resonant transmissions
You were sending outward into the aether
I was with you on that journey, Amigo
Trust me ~ there was no Mezcal

You were quietly starting a revolution
Smiling the whole damn time
Trying to conceal your laughter
Mostly because you were aware
Just how low
Under the radar
You were rolling

Dick Cheney
Is reclining in first class
With worn-out, tired blondes
   And a martini
 As you
   As you
     As you
Stand another stage
Making specific gestures
  Stretch yourself

  Stretch yourself
Make yourself *absolutely* clear

My erotic life
is seasonal
Out on the street
And looking
So self-aware
It's killing me
I can't stand myself
And yet
For now
I have to

Variation on a theme No. 2

The Robot Revolution will not be televised.
It will not be brought to you courtesy of 'Whole Foods Market', 'Greenpeace' or 'Rank Xerox'

The Robot Revolution will not be televised.
It will be sublime.

The Robot Revolution will not make you closer with God, your neighbor, or benefit alien intelligence via, anal probes, social understanding or your ability to refinance your home or have a larger penis.

The Robot Revolution will not be apart of some vast human conspiracy to stomp on your dreams, cancel your favorite shows or make you feel more apart of the masses than apart of the elite.

The Robot Revolution will not include drug use, talking during birth, catholic prayer or respect for anything caught in the bounds of everyday life, open information and men who fertilize a woman standing greater than five foot four.

The Robot Revolution will be lead by Tom Cruise driving a Lexus with a mentally deranged woman whom he would be calling 'his wife' during a would-be commercial.

The robot revolution will be led by Tom Cruise and will include the complete annihilation of our civilization in THX, DTS, 5.1 Dolby Surround and the powers that be will seek to preserve the Aspect Viewing Ratio in 16:1 to facilitate a greater close-up of our living savior, our man-on-the-beat, our five-four Alpha.

Bless us, O Mapother, for these thy gifts, which we are about to receive from Thy bounty. Through Cruise, our Lord we pray. Amen.

Hang up the phone
You'll be eaten by sharks
They have no mercy

I'm on hold
In-def
Long distance contacts erode
Phone call of the Uncool

Mister, I met a man, once …


Hello, Ugarte
   I'm watching *Casablanca* again …
      Don't worry
         I own it

It's still early march yet
It doesn't feel like winter at all
Los Angeles is on fire
Don't pay no mind though
It happens all the time
Didn't you read "*Miss Lonelyhearts*"?

No, they don't sell it at Target.

In 1942 they filmed for three months
   that now
      seem to be lasting forever

"Is that your favorite movie?"
   You know the answer.
      Must you ask?


*"The plane to Lisbon, you'd like to be on it."*
   Yes, I know all the words, too.
      I've seen it hundreds of times by now


Rick's always drinking brandy
   and smoking cigarettes
      It's quite a surprise
         that I don't have lung cancer
            or cirrhosis of the liver


I've always been a sucker for a good role model

I won't lie though,
   Every time I watch this
      An Absinthe bottle seems to surface
         I know for a fact now
            I'm very slowly being poisoned by the stuff

I don't believe there'll be any lessons tonight
Just a fantasy of
A white sport-coat
  and maybe
    A pink carnation

I repeat 'fantasy'
As if I expect their to be others.

However –
I have only one
And it keeps repeating unfaded in dark hallways
Of the past
In the closed office buildings of my mind

Maybe it's the Absinthe
Maybe it's Miss Ilsa Lund
Maybe it's you

The Absinthe is real
Ilsa's long dead
And you're long gone

There's a note
   That I left in my apartment
      You'll know where to find me

4am …

I've always preferred night
It's easier to remember the contours of your face in the darkness.
I see you more clearly then the music that sits on my piano.
The noise and distraction of my small apartment
Washed away your voice forever and cannot be reclaimed.

My mind tells me that you're like a young Faye Dunaway, close-up, smiling
Seductively, touching and pursing your lips tenderly.

At night I can see almost every detail of you.
Even the sharpened look in your eye
And the rise of your delicate female frame breathing.

Almost another lifetime now, but I seemed to have painted your memory with indelible ink, or fast drying cement.

My mind can reproduce the image of your face like a Xerox copier, every time identical.

Trust me, it's a blessing. It's enough.

Bob's Big Boy at 2am ...


These assholes aren't insomniacs.
They're vegetables that have been exposed to
too much sunlight and designer drugs.

You're just cattle, astray from the grazing pasture
and meandering blindly down the two-lane.
In my face and on my turf.

Sheep milling around the back of the shearing barn,
unaware that this time they'll be butchered at dawn,
instead of the usual quick ensemened raping.

My toast comes, and you guffawed.
My coffee came, and you snorted.
When the bacon comes will you have
a fucking break-down?

So, get out of my face with your television afflictions
that you're masking as something else to impress me.
A diagnosis encased in lethargy, masturbation and
white-trash delusions of Wal-Mart.

You're just searching for the next party and someone to puke on.
The disease you have is being alive and never having lived.

You're a waste of breath, the years you've spent
And a waste of breath the years behind.

You're just a bunch of fucking animals.
        The clubs are closed ... so go home.

I've drawn upon myself for years
And have often been left empty
I've learned to exist in the ashes
While breathing sand

Wiping my ass with a campaign hat
It scrapes across my backside like
Rice paper and
Kwai Chang Kane

Surrounded in the dark
Aroma of gut funk
My anus explodes like Baghdad in the night

I'll place bets on the filthy fuck
That finger-banged
My hot chocolate at 3:52am
@ my local Big Boy

Goddamned turd burglers
Slipping into the dusk
With my tip money
And another disenfranchised
Smug smirk

You're a fucking jerk, pal.
Your momma should've aborted you.

There have been nights
When I was so tired –
When I had barely closed my eyes
When my head has just touched down
My body exhausted

When the boats of my dreams departed
When the seas appear and
I find myself just as quickly awoken
To a pillow-fight and laughter and your face

And then …
Sunshine and the smell of coffee
Always breaks it upon the dawn
Shattering the moment

There's a longing in my heart
Pulling me back
Sinking deeper in

A thousand times
I've had this dream
Every waking moment
The pain of this reality
Is just as stabbing

A loss greater than a whole army
Of men in a futile battle

I don't know how to tell you

Hello Ivory Tower …

I'm knocking … it's me.
An old friend, the unlearned vagabond
rising from the gutter slowly to hand in my submission,
my body of work, my body,
my statement prima face.

I just want you to know …

I hope you take it all in and consider it.
For this sound will not rattle thine windows in the frame again for some time to come.

So get you hence to your seats and judge me, reject me, dispose of my thoughts for the recycling.

For it is your will and not mine that will shape the horses hooves in the receiving moment of this fading life.

Time to cut it adrift …


I'm going over the edge this year
And there's not a goddamned thing that you'll be able to say about it

Say what you like
It'll make no difference

But I'll be long gone by morning

I spent the entire year previous
Completely sober
That alone should be worth the cost of admission
Into the strangest trip on earth.

I have only a few things to say before I depart:
    I loved several women
    And in the end, I could've masturbated
    I spent a lot of money on foolish things
    And most of them still clutter my
    Two bedroom apartment
    Like a Vegas Nightmare

I'll never be free of most my baggage
As your Attorney, I advise you to burn everything.

The pain in my chest
Sometimes real
Sometimes imagined
Never goes away

I guess I'm just one of those
Who wish
They'd never been born at all

Fleeting moments of happiness
That I have trapped in my mind
As a collection of momentary photographs

Now, a grand total of
Almost
Ten seconds

I don't know about you
But I can't say it's enough

The Government has gone mad
And the country is in a fucking shambles
The baby boomers are breathing hard
Hoping Richard Nixon doesn't appear from the mist
To assume power
All over

Talking heads are killing everything
Within their reach
And crapping on anything
Within their grasp

George Bush is building a crown
From the bones of the poor and disenfranchised

Corporations are in love with illegal immigrants
Purchasing clothes, cars and one-way ticket bus fares
For their sacred journey to the promise land
Of Grease and Money

A world where Adam Sandler looks like Bob Dylan
And Dick Cheney makes Darth Vader
Look like Magnum P.I.

They're selling Keanu Reeves action figures
Just down the street to little kiddies and
Deformed adults that should be euthanized
Instead of institutionalized

Hillary Clinton is churning together
Mashed political gruel
From inexperienced politicians who are being stroked
For their future assassinations
   which will
      Keep the masses quiet
      Keep the Prozac coming
      And launch the missiles
      that are now gathering dust upon the lawn
      of every well-groomed, honey-combed suburb

Will there be a day
That will pass
And I will not see your face
Emblazoned upon every crevice of my mind, smiling?
In my dreams, near me?
In my past, laughing?

Words your father said ...


Here ya go, craphound
            Go play in traffic

Find a bridge to sleep under
            Curl up in a warm spot

Panhandle deadbeats
            In a downtown shelter

Trading stamps for cash
            With your social-worker

Hold your daddy tight

            That old sick joke
                In a hotel room shower
                    Got a smoke?
                        Got a light?

Variation on a theme No. 3


The iPod revolution will not be televised.
I will not be brought to you by Bill Gates, Steve Jobs or Bono.
It will not free your mind, free your soul or open your legs.
The iPod revolution will not be televised
It will be subscribed.

The iPod revolution will not be televised
It will not be brought to by Cake, Led Zeppelin or the dead ghost
of James Douglas Morrison.

Walt Whitman will not be pod-cast across Walden Pond
Jessica Tandy will not be pod-cast across Golden-Pond
And Blak Coke will only keep you up late
Watching re-runs of MASH, The Golden Girls and Conan O'Brian.

The iPod Revolution will not be televised
You will be bribed.

You cannot allot yourself more time to
Do the things you want like:
Reload your Nano or
Reload your AK-47 with 7.62mm ammo
Nick Cage & Peter Gabriel won't be able to describe the horror
Of a million unheard souls, helpless and
Plugged into a million downloaded albums and badly written,
badly preformed books-on-tape about how to get rich on e-bay,
selling homes quickly and taking a boatload of penis enlargement medicines.

None of these things will save you, free your mind, free your soul or open your legs

The iPod revolution will not be televised
It will be prescribed.

Haiku's from the past-life …


Got to hell, asshole
I don't give a fuck, okay?
Go piss up a rope



Fuck off, cocksucker
I want my fucking money back
That's not a movie



Pucker up, sweetheart
Suck my knob, down to the base
And hold! At the root



I'm about to crap
When you talk, my stomach aches
Surrounded by shit



Get in the damn grave
In my way, taking up space
Take your trash and split



I crapped on your grave
Desecrated my anus
Wiping with flowers

Observations of a Dead man
On a foreign shore
Looking back across the vast ocean
Standing transfixed
Upon the beach

Every Single Soul
Clinging desperately to its shell
In the world tonight
Everything is absolutely
Backwards

I can see myself
From where I stand
I'm fumbling around, lost
Searching … Still alive
Trying to find some way home

Ode to Irwin …


Departed by Ray not Croc
I was sitting at McDonalds
Staring at a bronzed picture of Ray Kroc

My phone rang several times
Letting me know you bolted
I was ready, my esophagus folded
Your heart had spiked, deflated

My arteries hardened
As yours constricted.
My mouth was engorged with hot burger
You, the Regulator, blood and salt water

When I came out for air
You didn't

They hauled you in with a hook
I sat stunned, digesting the information
You were instantly divesting your accumulations

In fear of dangling little Bob as bait
The docile Sting Ray maneuvered a sang-froid fate

I passed ten people
   While trying to buy groceries
Hearing their thoughts
  I heard several people thinking the following:

      *I think I'm going to slit my wrists*

      *My brother died in a car crash on the five*

      *I don't have enough money to pay the rent*

      *He's such a fucking liar*

      *They finally repossessed the truck*

      *Los Angeles is a goddamned cesspool*

      *That cunt gave me herpes*

      *The sunlight in this town gives me headaches*

      *Shit, I left my wallet in the car*

      *He's always forcing himself on me, I hate him.*

      *Fuck that guy, who the hell wears pink, anyway?*

My Neighbor happens to be
An Unfrozen Neanderthal
Classic red-neck genus
Scar tissue for brain
A child molester in waiting
State sponsored boarding is being built
He's pouring his own concrete
His destiny has stopped debating
His ego finds new ways of inflating
The self esteem is only bottled, a domestic imitation
A crap veneer on a Sunland exterior
White trash with horses to him seem superior
Everyone's waiting for his own tired-face to flush him
All bets are laid
All winners paid

When the gates open
Take aim

Lost in a haze
of Doughnuts
Found in an isle of
Processed foods
Mentally absent from
An overdose of
Milwaukee Ice, Pabst Blue ribbon,
Wild Turkey and
The sound of all our lives
Flushing deeply
Into the Porcelain Void

*'The way I see it'* is a series of poems that were submitted to the Starbucks Corporation in 2005 for a campaign to print the disposable, over-caffeinated ramblings of the general public's thoughts for the side of their coffee cups. Needless to say, nothing I ever sent them ever made it past the censors.

Strip-malls in the mist ...

The way I see it,
strip-malls were never considered as a cool or hip place to commune.
Historically seen as a blight on the horizon, a blemish on the landscape.
No one would've ever expected the strip-mall to be the seat of a revolution.
A culture clash of ideals, architecture and irony.
Who would've ever thought you'd have this revelation?
Who would've ever thought you would've participated
In this revolution?

Miles Davis at 4 am …

The way I see it,
I've been asleep my whole life,
but I know I've listened to that Miles Davis record at least a hundred times.
I've awoken confused, in a cold sweat before dawn,
believing I'd heard the creamy tones of his tenor-sax.
Was it inspiration shaking me, or something else?
It's at that moment, on the periphery of consciousness
that I'm most awake.

Enjoy 1989 …

The way I see it,
we spend entirely too much time in the past.
It seems like yesterday that I sat terrified on that recital stage in music class.
That was 1989.

Now, everywhere I turn,
every uncomfortable moment of my youth has been glorified,
sold and repackaged in every format possible.

What I can tell you now, is to just enjoy the product.

Operator …

The way I see it,
I can get into a lot of trouble on the telephone.

Sometimes, unknowingly,
I've dialed the number of the last person on earth
I ever wanted to talk with.

That can happen when you let yourself get distracted.

I've said things to telemarketers that could make a gaggle of pirates blush
and curtsy.
Stakes are high when you're ready to disconnect.

Last Supper ...


The way I see it,
I must've committed suicide about eight or nine times already.
Each time I went out like a gas lamp in a windstorm, or a bug against an open flame.
Combusting and falling toward the earth like a war protestor,
Protesting life, ingesting death like my last supper.

There I am, cooling on the heels of exhaustion,
only to get up, shake myself off, and try it again.

Propaganda at 10,000 feet …

The way I see it,
the mile-high club is over-rated.
It's nothing more than propaganda from profiteers
that would give us urban-sprawl, urban-blight,
strip-malls, strip-shows, industrial theme-parks,
corporate greed, embezzlement,
fraud, waste and abuse.

Everything unwholesome at ten-thousand feet
glamorized with a price tag and the promise
of something that can never be delivered,
confined to a space that can never be maneuvered.

Hyphenated Landscapes …


The way I see it,
Los Angeles has already sunk into the ocean.
I'm swimming in debt and neck-deep and gagging
on the fetid masses of poverty-stricken unfortunates
who are struggling to dog-paddle towards
ever-sinking islands of salvation and supposed paradise.
A sea layered in lottery tickets, adult day-cares and middle-aged madness
sinking deeper inside their four-wheel mid-life crisis.

Momentary Heartbreak …

The way I see it,
there are times in life when we absolutely make the wrong decision,
and from that there's just no coming back.
You know exactly what I'm speaking of.
The one you love, the one that's gone,
and the one that you'll just never see again.
All that heartbreak in that one moment, every time.
You proceed to convince yourself that everything will go your way.

The Abyss …

The way I see it,
some men think that they're invincible,
and no amount of sloth or vice will ever breed it out of them.
What is it about danger that makes some seek it out so desperately
as if it were the last breath of fresh air?
I would like to spend the currency of my life
on a suicide endeavor contrived by lunatics.

Intrigued?

From The Past ...


The way I see it,
I've been dead for about eleven years.
I awoke one evening in a black void
sometime in the middle of October of 1994.

I wonder if that date had any significance on any calendar?
I opened my eyes to the brightest light imaginable.
It was the lights of a truck outside my window.
Did I awake from a dream or the passage from life?

Midnight …

The way I see it,
being afraid of the dark isn't really a bad thing.
The accepted truth is that you're alone in bed, covered in with your fear.
In the midst of sleep, I've heard voices talking to me,
footsteps in my room and felt the brush of something beside me.
Being too paralyzed to move,
should I take comfort in the fact that I'm not alone?

Five-fifteen ...

The way I see it,
I'm still on active duty, on a mission.
Awaiting confirmation.
My nerves are like a crushed pack of cigarettes.
I keep staring at the phone, thinking it's about to ring.
I duck as I pass the windows, inside my own house.
I look at the clock at the same time everyday.

**Index of first lines ...**

| | |
|---|---|
| A prelude to a world gone mad | 30 |
| A note to Frank Reardon ... | 33 |
| Again ... | 38 |
| Anjelica Huston ... | 18 |
| Bob's Big Boy at 2am | 49 |
| Consciously Becoming | 01 |
| Crispin Hellion Glover ... | 42 |
| Dead Mexican Artist ... | 11 |
| Desperate | 24 |
| Enjoy 1989 ... | 69 |
| Every time I look in the mirror | 04 |
| Everything is just beyond my reach | 39 |
| Five-fifteen ... | 78 |
| 4am ... | 48 |
| From The Past ... | 76 |
| Fulang-Chang and I ... | 35 |
| Haiku's from the past-life ... | 60 |
| Hang up the phone | 45 |
| Hello Ivory Tower ... | 53 |
| Here I am watching 'Hannibal' | 36 |
| Hyphenated Landscapes ... | 73 |
| I need to tell you | 13 |
| In my other life I was | 16 |
| I passed ten people | 63 |
| I'm going to blow my brains out | 12 |
| I'm waiting for my heart to give out | 25 |
| I've always wanted to be a priest | 32 |
| I've drawn upon myself for years | 50 |
| I want to time travel back to 1951 | 19 |
| J.S. Bach is rolling in his grave | 31 |
| Just West of Unabomber ... | 17 |
| Klieg Light ... | 14 |
| Last Supper ... | 71 |
| Lawsuit ... | 37 |
| Lost in a haze | 65 |
| Martha, My Dear ... | 15 |
| Midnight ... | 77 |
| Miles Davis at 4 am ... | 68 |
| Mister, I met a man, once ... | 46 |
| Momentary Heartbreak ... | 74 |
| My erotic life | 43 |
| My Neighbor happens to be | 64 |
| My Wiener Dog ... | 28 |
| My wife Mini | 26 |

| | |
|---|---|
| Observations of a Dead man | 02 |
| Observations of a Dead man (reprise) | 61 |
| Ode to Irwin … | 62 |
| Operator … | 70 |
| Out on the fray … | 23 |
| Paul Weller & God … | 34 |
| Propaganda at 10,000 feet … | 72 |
| Poetry is a code | 10 |
| So, Keith Merritt wrote that poem | 27 |
| Sometimes I'd rather drink Mezcal … | 08 |
| Strip-malls in the mist … | 67 |
| Thank God for Bill Burroughs | 40 |
| The Abyss … | 75 |
| The Government has gone mad | 56 |
| The pain in my chest | 55 |
| The Pig-Bed … | 41 |
| The Pitch Black Lifetime … | 20 |
| There have been nights | 52 |
| This is me … is that you? | 05 |
| Time to cut it adrift … | 54 |
| Variation on a theme No. 2 | 44 |
| Variation on a theme No. 3 | 59 |
| We don't always lose … | 22 |
| Will there be a day | 57 |
| Words your father said … | 58 |
| Why do I believe in brotherhood? | 09 |
| Wiping my ass with a campaign hat | 51 |
| You can feel the transfer | 03 |

Born in Pennsylvania in 1971 and raised in England and various parts of Alaska. Attended school at the University of Alaska, Anchorage and the University of Los Angeles, California.

Steffan has lived in many places across the globe with a purpose bent on never being a tourist in his own home, town or country. Once a resident of Alaska, the Mayor of Nome, John Handelin, asked him to 'leave and never return', due to a minor misunderstanding.

He has been oft quoted as being an alien in all environments, unable to find his true home. He is disliked by most, but loved enough. He has an undying love of physics, literature and Caravaggio.

www.ingramcontent.com/pod-product-compliance
Lightning Source LLC
Chambersburg PA
CBHW031414040426
42444CB00005B/558